www.sugarfreelife.co.uk

Week 1 Day 1 Welcome

Hello and welcome to sugar-free in 28 days.
Thank you for joining me.

I am so excited to go on this journey with you and I congratulate you for deciding to work on your relationship with sugar.

It takes some time and effort but it is worth it. Imagine enjoying eating, being around food and being completely relaxed.

It does feel good, right?

I would suggest that you start on Saturday

This way you can prepare for the upcoming week without pressure.

The best practice is to watch a lesson in the morning, then during the day, you practice what I am asking you for that day. And download any tools provided in the lessons.

In this first 28 days it is vital that you take as much sugar out of your diet as possible. It's hard for the first 2 weeks. You will make mistakes and have difficult times but unlike diets it gets easier over time.

The key is this, be mindful, slow down and think. And if things go wrong, don't worry just start again.

Mondays, we'll talk about food, food that is going to help you to have fewer cravings.

Tuesdays, we will talk about cravings and tools that you could use to overcome cravings.

Wednesdays, we'll talk about mindfulness and mindful eating.

Thursdays about stress and what stress actually does to you and what you can do about it.

Fridays, we'll talk about habits and how to build them.

Saturdays, I would like you to go back and review the week

Sundays we completely forget about the world and pay attention to yourself. Self-care and prep for the next week.

Sugar free Life

Questionnaire

Before you start

1. What is your name?

2. How old are you?

3. Have you tried to stop eating sugar before?

4. How long did you stop for?

5. Why did you start eating sugar again?

6. Have you ever been on a diet?

7. Are you happy with your weight?

8. What medication do you take?

9. How is your digestion?

10. How well do you sleep?

11. How high are your energy levels?

12. What exercise do you take?

13. Do you suffer with stress?

Sugar free Life

Questionnaire

Before you start continued . . .

14. Do you have mood swings?

15. Brain Fog?

16. Do you have any food allergies?

17. Do you suffer with depression?

18. How's your menstrual cycle?

19. Do you get constipated?

20. Are you under a doctors care?

21. Do you have any thyroid issues?

22. Are you diabetic/having tests?

23. Do you take supplements?

24. Do you have treatment with steroids?

25. Have you had/are having chemotherapy?

26. Are you a fast, moderate or slow eater?

27. What do you eat for breakfast?

28. At what time is breakfast?

Questionnaire

Before you start continued . . .

29. What do you eat for lunch?

30. What time is lunchtime?

31. What do you eat for dinner?

32. What time is dinner time?

33. Do you eat snacks?

Your notes and thoughts before you begin the course

Day 2 ME TIME

Sugar free in 28 Days

Top Tips for Week One

- Take all the sugar out of your house

- Write your Why

- Check the list of food you need for the following week and add more if you need to

- Do your food shopping today

- SLOW DOWN

- Self-care – ME TIME – have a bath with some essential oils, go for a walk, read a book, see a friend, meditate . . .

Sugar free Life

Day 2 What is my WHY?

Say it with love, with compassion. You are your greatest support. Be there for you.

Record your why on your phone. Listen daily, at list once a day and any time you have cravings.

Week 1 Food Diary

Download the 7 Day Sample Meal Plan - Then write here what you actually had

Day 1

Breakfast

Lunch

Dinner

Day 2

Breakfast

Lunch

Dinner

Day 3

Breakfast

Lunch

Dinner

Day 4

Breakfast

Lunch

Dinner

Sugar *free* Life

Week 1 Food Diary

Be honest about what you actually had

Day 5

Breakfast

Lunch

Dinner

Day 6

Breakfast

Lunch

Dinner

Day 7

Breakfast

Lunch

Dinner

My Notes

*Be honest, note everything, sit down to eat, focus on your meals, eat only what is on the recommended list

Sugar free Life

Day 2 Downloads

Download the Don't Eat & Recommended Foods Lists - Or refer to them here

Don't Eat List

Beans / Legumes	Fruits except berries	Potato
Rice	Corn	Sugars / syrups / honey
Soy, corn, canola oil	Lean or low fat foods	Trans Fats (Hydrogenated)
Grains	Processed Meat	Alcohol
Fruit Juice	Artificial Sweeteners	Sugar added (ex, in Peanut Butter)

Just because it's not on this list doesn't mean you can have it - always check the label - sugar in it, can't have it! Time to do some research.

Recommended Foods List - Non-Starchy Vegetables

Parsley	Aubergine	Bell Peppers
Asparagus	Mushrooms	Garlic
Lettuce - Iceberg / Romaine	Collard Greens	Brussels Sprouts
Green Beans	Cauliflower	Cucumber
Spinach	Kale	Celery
Radish	Courgette	Bok Choi
Arugula	Broccoli	Cabbage
Bean Sprouts		

You will eat more fats here, some proteins, a lot of fruit and veg, but this is not Atkins, or other similar fads, this is lifelong healthy eating with good foods and habits.

Recommended Foods List - Fats

Avocado Oil	Butter	Coconut Butter
Coconut Milk	Coconut Oil	Ghee
Lard	Heavy Whipping Cream	Mayonnaise
Olive Oil	Sour Cream	Safflower Oil
Tallow		

Healthy fat can actually help you lose weight, don't be afraid of fats

Sugar free Life

Day 2 Downloads

Download the Don't Eat & Recommended Foods Lists - Or refer to them here

Recommended Foods List - Other Carbs

Artichokes	Avocado	Almonds
Beetroot	Blackberries	Blueberries
Brazil Nuts	Carotts	Cashew Nuts
Chia Seeds	Hazelnuts	Flax Seeds
Hemp Seeds	Hummus	Lemons
Limes	Macadamia Nuts	Olives
Onions	Peanuts	Pecans
Pine Nuts	Pistachio Nuts	Pumpkin Seeds
Raspberries	Strawberries	Sunflower Seeds
Tomatoes	Walnuts	

Recommended Foods List - Proteins

Bacon	Cheese	Chicken
Eggs	Fish	Minced beef
Steak	Ham (unglazed)	Lamb
Pork	Salami	Shrimp / Prawns
Turkey		
My Favourites		

You won't find strict rules here, when you put in a little effort then you commit more, better committed, better results, got it?

Sugar free Life

Week 1 - My Shopping List

Day 3 Food

Healthy Fats and Carbs

Healthy fat can actually help you lose weight, don't be afraid of fats

Lesson 1

This course is all about how to reduce sugar cravings.

To have fewer sugar cravings, eat healthy fats.

Healthy fats would be: nuts, seeds, olive oil, avocado, oily fish, organic butter...

Why is that?

Simply because those foods are going to keep your blood sugar level stable.

When you eat healthy fat your blood sugar levels become stable. It's much easier not to have sugar cravings and you feel better. No will power needed or you need less.

You want to stay away from carbs, but not any carbs, just the carbs that have a high content of sugar, especially processed carbs, such as pasta and pizza. Also, potatoes and rice have a high content of sugar so reduce it or stay away from it, if you can.

Do not be afraid of fat, please. It is NOT going to make you fat. Actually healthy fat makes you lose weight.

If you're here because you want to lose weight don't think about it right now. Our goal is to reduce sugar cravings and stop eating sugar. That on its own is going to give you the results you want.

At the end of this program, you will see **the weight will go down.**

If you are unsure about the sugar content of any foods, you can always Google it and find out what it is. Choose foods with a low sugar content.

Just follow, trust in the process, do your best and be honest when you complete your food diary for each week.

Sugar free Life

Day 4 Cravings

and what to do about them

Have you recorded your why? Do it and listen to it whenever temptation strikes

Lesson 2

Your cravings are probably quite high today and that is normal, and ok.

You may have have a really big problem for about three to five days, and then it gets easier.

After 10 days life becomes easier. You will start to feel benefits like better mood, more energy better sleep and more.

Willpower is limited, what you want is to expose yourself less to the temptations and also use the techniques that I am going to share with you. Like a detective, you are starting to look for your triggers. Sometimes that is not easy and that is OK. You are learning a new skill. If you need help get in touch.

Next time a situation provokes you into eating something you know is high in sugar, that you reach for to make you feel better, or punish yourself with, just stop for a moment. Think about these things:

1. What is it that triggered me?
2. What could I do differently to deal with this trigger and the way it has made me feel?

This journey is not easy when you are on your own - it is OK to ask for help - contact me if you need support.

On the following pages find the details of the steps to begin practicing today and a section to record your triggers.

Sugar free Life

Day 4 Actions

Things to practice today

Action 1: First when the craving comes, recognise it.

What is this that I'm feeling right now?

Am I: bored, lonely, need a hug, really hungry, tired, angry, sad, need more energy, or something else?
You need to identify what it is that you are feeling, use the triggers page to capture your thoughts and actions.

Action 2: Take a slightly deeper and longer breath in. Do it 3 times.

Take the few seconds needed to do this, it gives you time to step away from the trigger.

Now say to yourself, as you continue to breathe deeply,

  "I am going to have the sugar later if I still want it, but I'm not going to have it now".
Then go and do something else.

Action 3: Pick up your phone and listen to your why

Listening to your own voice reminding you why you are doing this, your own reasons for creating a healthier, better life for yourself, is incredibly powerful as a motivator.

Action 4: Visualisation - Feeling that you have a choice is powerful

Close your eyes and imagine your body. Now imagine you took that sugary food that you feel cravings for.
Imagine your liver; how much work does it have to do to process that sugar?
Think of the sugar flowing through your bloodstream, Your pancreas leaping into action to create the insulin needed to deal with that sugar in your blood.
Your heart now needs to pump harder, your brain loses memory capability the more sugar you eat.
Your brain starts to age faster. Your body will age faster.
You get maybe 15 minutes of satisfaction as your blood sugar spikes, then the insulin brings it down again. Then your blood sugar level is unbalanced and you begin craving again.
Time to stop the cycle. You have a choice.
Stop and breathe, leave it until later, do something else.
Your whole body will benefit and that means you will benefit.
You might record this exercise on your phone so you could listen when you need support.

Sugar free Life

Day 4 Triggers

Record here your triggers, how they make you feel, and how you can deal with them in a way that doesn't involve high sugar food to make you feel better or punish yourself

Trigger 1

The Situation, event or occurence that triggers you

How does it make you feel?

What can you do to avoid or deal with the trigger other than eat high sugar foods?

If you haven't recorded your why on your phone yet then **do it now**!

Trigger 2

The Situation, event or occurence that triggers you

How does it make you feel?

What can you do to avoid or deal with the trigger other than eat high sugar foods?

Print out this page as many times as you need to so that you capture all your triggers

Sugar free Life

Day 5 Mindful Eating

And it's role in helping you to stop eating sugar

Lesson 3

We are going to talk about mindfulness and mindful eating. Let's see what that has to do with our work. Our goal is to stop eating sugar.

The question is why do we eat sugar in the first place? As I said before will power is a very limited resource. The more you use it during the day the less is left. That is the reason why in the evenings, we go for the worst behaviour.

We are creatures of habit and we do many things without consciously thinking about it. When we want to make a change **we need to bring what is unconscious into the conscious mind** – to become aware. Then we can change the behaviour.

I would like to give you 7 steps for Mindful Eating.

The first two are detailed on the next page, the rest will come over the next three weeks of lessons.

Mindfulness is such a powerful practice. You will get to know yourself better and better.

You will start to first notice and then see that you have a choice. Then you choose the behaviour.

A powerful skill to have. It takes time to develop but it is worth it.

Sugar free Life

Day 5 Mindful Eating

Here are the first two of the seven steps to mindful eating for you to practice today

Mindful Eating Technique 1

First - eat only when you're sitting

- You take the plate, put the food on the plate and sit at your dinner table.
- The interesting thing is that when you need to sit down, instead of walking and binging you start thinking: should I eat this? Do I really want to?
- This is a great way to avoid mindless eating where you pick up some food in the kitchen, eat it without thinking for a second about it. When you need to sit down, it's completely different, something happens, you become aware.

Mindful Eating Technique 2

The second part is to avoid all distractions.

What do we normally do?
- We would eat and read emails, watch the news, look at the phone, answer the emails...
- We are multitasking, thinking we don't want to waste time just eating. We have so many tasks. We need to do blah, blah, blah, blah, blah.
- When you do other things while eating you don't pay any attention to the food or your body. If you eat like that you will eat more than your body needs. Body send signals, giving you feedback to stop but you don't listen.

How about stopping this mindless eating.
- I would like you to become mindful about your food because your body is telling you when the food you're eating is not good for you or it is time to stop eating but if you're paying attention to everything else, there is nobody at home to hear the message, right?
- This is about becoming a friend with your body, understanding when the body is giving you pain or discomfort you listen.
- I have quite a few clients who had digestion problems. When they started practising mindful eating digestion improved and with some completely went away.

Even if you're short with time when you do this you will see benefits:
- Your body will digest your food better
- You will be able to have more energy and feel better
- You will be more productive when you get back to work so you are not wasting your time

Sugar free Life

Day 6 Stress

Stress level is in direct correlation with your sugar cravings

Lesson 4

When the stress level is high sugar cravings also go up for most of us. How about you?

- Do you eat sugar when you are stressed?
- Do you think something is wrong with you?
- Do you want to push it down, suppress it, resist it?

Did you know that resistance brings stress up as well as our cravings for sugar? How about choosing something else instead of going for food/sugar?

A lot of people are using food for stress reduction. What about you?

Today I would like to talk about sleep, and it's impact on your stress.

When you don't have enough sleep, you're lacking energy. When you're lacking energy, the fastest way for the body to bring that energy up is to make you eat some sugar, because it is the fastest way to bring the energy up. The body is clever. When you are tired you will probably grab either coffee, something sweet or both, but none of those to resolve the problem. It is a short term solution.

What we are trying to learn in this course over and over again, is to look at what the problem is, deal with a problem, so you don't need to go for sugar again. If sleep is your problem, then you need to address it.

See tips on getting proper sleep on the next page, and remember to download the guided meditation.

Sugar free Life

Day 6 Stress

Tips to help you improve your sleep

Tip 1   Try to unwind before you go to bed

If you keep thinking and thinking about problems, your brain just keeps working. What about trying to meditate. List below what helps you to get relaxed:

Tip 2   Try to go to bed before 10pm

If that is too early for you try to go backwards 30 minutes . For example, If you're going to go to bed at 11.30, try to go at 11

Tip 3   Make your bedroom dark

Turn off the TV. If you must have light make it a soft, dim light, not too bright.

Tip 4   Think about temperature

You don't want to be hot. You don't want to be cold. It needs to be just right for you.

Tip 5   Turn off your screens

Stop looking at the screens 2 hours before bed, no phone, no TV, no laptop, because all of those are making your brain too active. A better option would be to read a book.

Tip 6   Gratitude practice

Be grateful for something that really happened to you today, feel it with your whole heart. My practice is to find 3 things that I am grateful for the day. If I do that just before I fall asleep, I'm going to sleep with nice positive thoughts, and that affects my sleep and my dreams. If I go with gratitude in my heart, chances are much higher that I will have a good relaxing sleep.

Tip 7   Don't eat within 3 hours before you go to bed

Because you might have problems with your digestion. And you will awake more energised.

Tip 8   Meditation

Meditation calms your brain, calms your mind, helps the mind let go of the thoughts, worries.

Tip 9   At least Relax

Even if you can't sleep do at least try doing things that help you to relax and unwind.

Sugar free Life

Day 7 Habits

Goals and Systems
Build new healthy habits to replace the old unhealthy habits
Lesson 5

When we want to change something, make an improvement, do something new, we create a goal. We all do that.

Let me ask you a question: what's the difference between losers and winners?

Do they all have goals? Yes. So the goal is not the problem.

What is found in the research is that people who are winners have systems in place. That's the difference.

Now let's go back to you. You have a goal - **you want to stop eating sugar**.

You have your WHY, you have begun to follow the steps and actions in this course. The system that works. For everyone in different ways. Stick with it.

It is important to practice all the tools I am teaching you on the course. Don't dismiss it without practise. At the end of 28 days you will know which tools were the best for you. Instead of ROOLS you will have your TOOLS.

You might not like some of the tools, but please, while the course is going on, follow what I recommend daily and see what feels good and what doesn't at the end of the course. Give it some time, please.

Today's task is to **avoid temptations**. See some ways how on the next page.

Sugar free Life

Day 7 Good Habits

Tips to help you improve your habits by avoiding temptation

Tip 1   Do Your Shopping on Sunday

To do this effectively, to avoid temptation takes planning.

1. Plan your meals for the week using the food lists and your research on what works for you that is sugar free / very low in sugar.
2. Make a list of all the foods you need for those meals and any healthy snacks you might want to include.
3. Stick to the list when you go shopping!

Tip 2   Avoid the temptation aisles

You know the ones: Crisps, sweets, biscuits, bread, alcohol, just don't go down them!

Tip 3   Avoid your temptation triggers

Stay away from the saboteur 'friend', you know the one; they find out you are trying to cut down, be healthy etc. and they do everything in their power to get you to have that cake or eat that donut, or have a double gin.

Surround yourself with healthy people who support your efforts.

Tip 4   Plan when you can't avoid

It isn't always possible to stay away from places and people that trigger your sugary food temptations but you can do a bit of avoidance planning.

Parties: Have water between drinks and drink slowly, choose the healthy options from the buffet

Meals: Leave what you don't want, you are worth your efforts, people pleasing is not going to help you.

Coffee with friends: Black coffee or fruit tea instead of a full fat caramel latte!

My notes on temptation and how to avoid it

Sugar free Life

WEEK 2

Day 8 Practice

Repetition for Success
Review Day

Remember that Saturday is the day recommended for you to begin this course and we have come around to the second Saturday already!

On Saturdays, I would like you to go back and review the week.

I would like you to see what do you remember from the lessons.

Keep practising and practising.

If you need, go back to some or all the videos or transcripts.

It's up to you.

Make sure you have completed all the workbook activities this week.

On the next page you can capture any thoughts and notes that you want to ensure you don't lose as you move forwards.

Sugar free Life

My Notes Week 1

Day 9 Me Time

Rest, plan and reassess

Let's get ready for success in week 2

On Sundays I would like you to completely forget about the world and pay attention to you.

Self-care and prep for the next week.

The only work would be to make a plan of what are you going to eat next week.

If you can also buy the food so you can stay away from shops for the rest of the week.

So prepare.

Sugar free Life

Week 2 - My Shopping List

Week 2 Food Diary

Download the 7 Day Sample Meal Plan - Then write here what you actually had

Day 1

Breakfast

Lunch

Dinner

Day 2

Breakfast

Lunch

Dinner

Day 3

Breakfast

Lunch

Dinner

Day 4

Breakfast

Lunch

Dinner

Sugar free Life

Week 2 Food Diary

Be honest about what you actually had

Day 5

Breakfast

Lunch

Dinner

Day 6

Breakfast

Lunch

Dinner

Day 7

Breakfast

Lunch

Dinner

My Notes

*Be honest, note everything, sit down to eat, focus on your meals, eat only what is on the recommended list

Sugar free Life

Day 10 Food

Sweeteners
Lesson 6

I didn't mention sugar replacements in the first week, simply because I wanted your taste buds to forget the taste of sugar. Taste buds are changing quite quickly. Within 10 days your body doesn't really remember the taste of sugar.

Now I would like to talk about sweeteners that I recommend.

If you have time to make your own desserts, please do that because that's the best option, just stay away from wheat flour and sugar, obviously.

Replace sugar with a natural sweeteners that I will tell you a little bit more about.

The sweeteners that I recommend here are not affecting your blood sugar level at all. There are 3 I would like you to try:

Stevia - natural, made from plants.

Erythritol - is the one that I like to use for baking.

Xylitol-You have to be careful with it because some people might have an upset stomach

See more on the next page about sweeteners and how to use them.

Remember - net carbs under 3 grams when buying snacks and desserts

Day 10 FOOD

Main Sweeteners and how to use them *(see more info in the download)*

Erythritol is a sugar alcohols. It is low carb and has 0 net carbs. It is found in nature but has a glycemic index of 0 and is easy to digest. Sugar alcohols are not artificial sweeteners. There is some processing involved, but this is no less natural than the processing needed for coconut sugar or maple syrup. If you can, buy non-GMO and/or organic. Erythritol is naturally occurring in many fruits. It's made through simple fermentation. How to use erythritol: You'll need 1 1/3 cups of erythritol to replace 1 cup of sugar. It tastes like sugar. It may have a slight cooling-like aftertaste similar to mint. I haven't noticed that. You can use it in baking the same way as sugar. It is good to use it for muffins, cakes, pancakes, cookies, or anything than needs to crisp up when baked.

XYLITOL It is also sugar alcohol. Made by fermenting corn or birch. You need to be careful if you haven't tried it before because it can cause a small amount of stomach upset. It is usually fine in moderation. It is also keto friendly, 0 net carbs. It is as sweet as sugar and can be used as a 1:1 replacement. Tastes just like sugar and has no aftertaste! Xylitol can be used for baking, creates moist, soft-baked goods that don't need a crunch. It is good to use it for muffins, soft-baked cookies, ice cream and cakes. You can also use it for coffees and teas.

STEVIA Made from the stevia plant. Available in liquid and granulated form. It is low carb and has 0 net carbs. Something you are going to love about Stevia - it has some healthy benefits, such as anti microbial, anti-fungal, anti-tumor, anti-oxidant, and anti-diabetic. Stevia is extremely sweet so you have to be very carful when using it. It could have a bitter aftertaste so you need to try different brands and see which one you like. It is good for teas, coffee, smoothies and not so good for baking unless you mix it with other sweeteners.

ALLULOSE It is a natural sugar that can't be metabolised. 0 glycemic index and 0 net carbs. It is found in fruit, maple syrup, and other plants. Allulose is a new keto sweetener but it seems it is getting more popular. It is now available on UK market but it is not easy to find it. I haven't explored it myself so I am sharing what I found in literature. Similar to erythritol, it's made using a natural fermentation process. Since it's fermented from a plant, it's not considered an artificial sweetener. Similar to erythritol, it's made using a natural fermentation process. Since it's fermented from a plant, it's not considered an artificial sweetener. When using allulose, you will need 1 1/3 cup of allulose per 1 cup of sugar. Many people use it as a 1:1 substitute without noticing a difference. Tastes like sugar with no bitterness or aftertaste! Allulose is best in soft baked goods such as pancakes, muffins, soft-baked cookies, and cakes.

Sugar free Life

Day 11 Cravings 2

The Sedona Method
Lesson 7

Sedona is all about letting go.

We all know we should let go of many unwanted habits but somehow we are not doing it. We just keep holding on to the feelings that are keeping us stuck.

The problem is HOW to let go.

The way to explain how Sedona works is to imagine a pen in your hand. Just take a pen. Then hold it tightly. After a while, it feels uncomfortable, right?

The pen represents all our limiting beliefs, emotions, thoughts, all the things that we don't like to feel. Our hand is our awareness.

So tell me, is that pen connected to your hand?

Could you let it go?
Could you just drop it!
Does it feel hard to open your hand?

Could you turn your hand down and just drop the pen? Just let it drop by itself.

That's how most people explain what Sedona is and how it works.

Watch the session in the video for today to understand it better as a tool for reducing food cravings.

Day 11 Cravings 2

Record here the foods you crave most, how you feel about them on a scale of 1 to 10. Then use the Sedona Method and record how you feel afterwards on the same

Food 1:

How much do you want it (before)?

1	2	3	4	5	6	7	8	9	10
No Craving									Want it Now

Do the Sedona Method for this food now

How much do you want it (after)?

1	2	3	4	5	6	7	8	9	10
No Craving									Want it Now

My Thoughts

Food 2:

How much do you want it (before)?

1	2	3	4	5	6	7	8	9	10
No Craving									Want it Now

Do the Sedona Method for this food now

How much do you want it (after)?

1	2	3	4	5	6	7	8	9	10
No Craving									Want it Now

My Thoughts

Leave some time between each Sedona session otherwise you will get overwhelmed

Sugar free Life

Day 12 Mindfulness 2

Mindful Eating 2
Lesson 8

Today I want to add the next step: **Slow Eating - This is really powerful.**

First I need to ask you are you a slow, moderate or fast eater?
If you're a fast eater, this is not an easy skill for you, but you can do this.

I worked with a lot of clients who were eating fast and it was hard for them at the beginning. It took them weeks to master but It's worth it. It's a really good skill to have. A lot of people I worked with would start to eat less than before just by slowing down. Rather than cutting the portions, forcing yourself to eat less, you slow down.

When you slow down, you will eat less without trying, without doing anything about it. By slowing down you're also giving your brain a chance to give you feedback that it is time to stop. Other benefits of slow eating are: your digestion becomes better, you will feel better, you'll have more energy...

I would like you to keep observing what are you doing, **be a detective, mindful observer**, whatever you like to call it but start journaling.

You can write a lot if you like but you don't have to. You might just open your phone, pick up the notes and put a few words. Those words might be enough for you to remind you of what you discovered.

Whether you write a few words or several pages, do what feels right for you.

The next page is a journaling page for you to print out as many times as you need to create your journal.

Sugar free Life

Day 12 Mindfulness 2

My Journal

Day

My Thoughts

Day

My Thoughts

Day 13 Stress 2

Movement v Exercise
Lesson 9

Moving is what we want to achieve

I would like to make you aware of movement versus exercise. A lot of my clients love this approach. What do I mean? Whatever you were doing as an exercise keep doing.

It is important to know that your body really wants you to move. It doesn't have to be an exercise. Did you know until the 1950s gyms didn't exist?

When you exercise you go from one extreme to the other -You're sitting all day long and then you go to the gym for an hour and a half. So you're going from one to another extreme. That puts the body under a lot of stress.

Also, a lot of people want to reward themselves after that exercise with a piece of cake???

Tips for movement will follow on the next page.

The To-Do List and the Not-To-Do List
What do you have to do and what do you not have to do. Think about a healthy ritual.

Complete your lists using the page provided.

Meditation
I would recommend you try this https://mindfulyou.space/.

Sugar free Life

Day 13 Stress

Tips to help you improve your movement levels

Tip 1 Sitters - Stand Up

After every 50 to 60 minutes of sitting, either at work or just watching TV, stand up and move around for 10 minutes.

You can set up an alarm on your phone. When you hear an alarm you stand up and move any way you prefer. You could put the music on dance a little bit. Do what you enjoy doing not what you "should" be doing. If you do something you hate, it's going to be hard and it is not going to last.

Tip 2 Let's Shake

If something upsets you and you feel a bit nervous, some shaking is a good thing to do. Definitely reduces the stress.

My To Do List - Priorities for the Day

Task 1

Task 2

Task 3

Task 4

My NOT To Do List - Tasks I can delegate or postpone

Day 14 Habits 2

Consistency and Small Steps
Lesson 10

Every step In this course has a reason to be there. I developed this practice over years of working with clients. You have very short daily lessons. I am asking you to do only one or two actions a day. I want you to make small steps, but to stay consistent, and to keep coming back, look at the lessons, do what we said to do on any particular day and just keep moving slowly, but constantly.

When you're making small steps, your brain will resist less and give you more chances to achieve your goal. Your saboteur is not going to wake up and say, 'I can't do this. This is so hard' When steps are simple and small you can keep going. You're not bringing more stress. It feels simple and easy.

Be aware that it doesn't mean that you're not going to have bad days. You will have bad days and good days, and that's normal. That is part of the journey. This is not a linear process. It's more like a spiral.

The trend is that you are going upwards slowly and gradually. **When you do that slowly it's simple, easy and over time it could become effortless**. I've seen it many times before.

You can do this.

I would like you to think about anything that could make it easier for you to keep going, such as making your own desserts or maybe buying products I suggested this week. Stay away from sugar and make it really hard and complicated to go back to sugar. Make what you don't want complicated and hard. At the same time make it really easy and simple to do things that you want to keep developing. Use the table on the next page to help you do this.

Sugar free Life

Day 14 Habits 2

Consistency and Small Steps

Stuff I can do to help me keep going

1.

2.

3.

4.

5.

6.

7.

8.

9.

10.

11.

12.

13.

14.

Sugar free Life

WEEK 3

Day 15 Practice, Practice

Repetition for Success
Review Day

Like any other habit, your new routine gets easier over time. It is possible to make it effortless. I have seen it many times. The only way to make that happen is to make it a habit and to learn how to deal with cravings. That is the goal of this course – to help you become a person who doesn't eat sugar.

I would like to congratulate you for being here with me for 2 weeks.

If you didn't have any sugar for 2 weeks it is a big achievement, well done!!

If you couldn't resist sugar a few times I congratulate you anyway because you are still here. That means you want this.

You might need some support to help you stay on track. You can call a friend or you can get in touch with me. I would love to help you. Sometimes it is about having an accountability partner, or you might need to work on your emotional eating. It is not easy to work on that on your own.

It is OK to ask for help. Here is the link to book 30 minutes session with me: https://calendly.com/greenmindfulketo/30min

Keep practicing! Remember how hard it was when you were learning to drive? Is it hard now?

And download the meditation to help relieve any stress you have.

Sugar free Life

My Notes Week 2

Day 16 Me Time

Rest, plan and reassess
Let's get ready for success in week 3

Self care day

No lessons today.

Today I only would like you do 1 job - meal plan for next week.

It is best to do it in the morning and then enjoy the rest of the day.

Do something you really love.

Think about this as a recharging day.

Please don't go to finish your work.

 Don't read your emails.

It is important to rest and have fun otherwise you can't keep going.

Have a great day and see you tomorrow.

Sugar free Life

Week 3 - My Shopping List

Week 3 Food Diary

Download the 7 Day Sample Meal Plan - Then write here what you actually had

Day 1

Breakfast

Lunch

Dinner

Day 2

Breakfast

Lunch

Dinner

Day 3

Breakfast

Lunch

Dinner

Day 4

Breakfast

Lunch

Dinner

Sugar free Life

Week 3 Food Diary

Be honest about what you actually had

Day 5

Breakfast

Lunch

Dinner

Day 6

Breakfast

Lunch

Dinner

Day 7

Breakfast

Lunch

Dinner

My Notes

Be honest, note everything, sit down to eat, focus on your meals, eat only what is on the recommended list

Sugar free Life

Day 17 Food 3

Alcohol and Fruit Juice
Lesson 11

The first week, we talk about adding more healthy fats into your diet, such as nuts, seeds, avocados, oily fish, meat, eggs. Don't be afraid of eating more fat. Healthy fat is not going to make you bigger. On the contrary, to lose fat around your tummy, you need to add more healthy fat to your diet.

What you want to reduce are carbs. Not all carbs are equal. I would like you to avoid pasta, bread, bagels, rice, potato.

In the second week, I introduced some sweeteners which I like to use, which are healthy and natural. Hope you had a chance to play with some or all of those. I recommended 3: Stevia, Erythritol and Xylitol. You have the details about these in lesson 6.

Today we are adding 2 new subjects : alcohol and fruit juices.
Fruit juices are also not recommended, sorry. The sugar content in fruit juices is really high.

Adding more water and herbal teas helps. It is OK to drink coffee.

Quality of your food
Please download the Clean 15 and Dirty 12 list supplied in this lesson in terms of organic or not organic choices.

Go step by step and you WILL start to feel better, your mood will go up as well as energy and you will sleep better. Over time you will see the difference. Also, your journey gets easier and easier.

Sugar free Life

The Clean 15 & the Dirty 12

Organic or not organic

The "Dirty Dozen" To ALWAYS Buy Organic

1 Strawberries
2 Spinach
3 Nectarines
4 Apples
5 Peaches
6 Pears
7 Cherries
8 Grapes
9 Celery
10 Tomatoes
11 Sweet Bell Peppers
12 Potatoes

Some more foods to put on ALWAYS ORGANIC list: Leafy Greens, Coffee, Eggs, Meat, Dairy

The "Clean 15" You DON'T Need to Buy Organic

1 Sweet Corn (non-GMO)
2 Avocados
3 Pineapples
4 Cabbage
5 Onions
6 Sweet Peas
7 Papayas
8 Asparagus
9 Mangos
10 Aubergine
11 Honeydew Melon
12 Kiwi
13 Cantaloupe
14 Cauliflower
15 Grapefruit

More grocery items to the list of non-organic foods to purchase:
Melons, Citrus fruits, Bananas, Squashes, Quinoa, Maple Syrup

Day 18 Cravings 3

Noticing /call a Friend
Lesson 12

Today we are talking about cravings.

It is important to know that cravings will come back. Expecting cravings to go away is impossible. What is possible is to face the cravings, be with it and make a conscious choice of what to do about it.

First time you experience cravings coming up but choosing not to go for sugar is the milestone to gaining your power back. The more you do it the better it feels.

You stop being afraid of cravings.

Today we are adding 2 more techniques:

1. Noticing
&
2. Call a Friend

Please see the detail of these techniques on the next page

Day 18 Cravings 3

2 great techniques for overcoming cravings

Technique 1: Noticing - scale your craving from 1 to 10

Step 1   Notice and name 5 things you SEE around you

Step 2   Notice and name 4 things you can FEEL

Step 3   Name 3 things you can HEAR

Step 4   Notice and name 2 things you can SMELL

Step 5   Name 1 thing you can TASTE

Notice the intensity of your cravings now from 1-10.
If it is still high try the second technique - Call a friend.

Technique 2: Call a friend

Step 1   Make sure that you choose friends you trust who will support
you

Step 2   Train them before you start WHY you are doing this and how
you want them to help, what you want them to say to you

Step 3   When you are struggling, have cravings or just need support,
call one of your trained and trusted friends. And listen to
their advice! Don't wait, do it as soon as you feel the need
for support.

Sugar free Life

Day 19 Mindfulness 3

The Hunger and Fullness Scale
Lesson 13

Today we are talking about mindfulness and mindful eating.

The first five mindfulness techniques were:
1. Eat without distraction
2. Eat sitting at the table
3. Just notice your emotions
4. Eat slowly
5. Notice what is happening in your life and write it down

Toady we concentrate on 6. the hunger and fullness scale

Hunger

We may be physically hungry but we may actually be emotionally hungry. Physical hunger requires food (observing the first 5 mindfulness techniques).
Emotional hunger needs investigation. See the form on the next page to help you note whether you are emotionally hungry and what to do about it.

Scale

On a scale of 1 to 10 how hungry are you. Use this scale before every meal.
It's again about bringing awareness about food and also what's going on in your life when you eat emotionally. This is the process where you're going to learn to see the difference between real hunger and emotional hunger so you can start changing that and stop eating emotionally.

Day 19 Mindfulness 3

Understanding emotional hunger

If you are really physically hungry you will feel it in your tummy.

If you're emotionally hungry, you will feel it somewhere else in the body.

When you feel physical hunger any food will do the work. You're not very fussy about it.

When you want to eat very specific food usually it's about the emotion that you want to either bring in or get rid of. Try to notice the difference.

Obviously when you're physically hungry, please go and eat. If you are not physically hungry could you try to find what the emotion is behind your hunger?

What can you do about it? *(think what you did that worked)*

Scale how hungry you are 1 = not hungry and 10 = starving

Called a friend for support

Meditated until hunger went away

Drank a glass of water

Ask yourself : What do I really want?

Focused on what might be causing me to feel hungry

Other:

Other:

Other:

Other:

Sugar free Life

Day 20 Stress 3

Self Compassion
Lesson 14

Today we are talking about how to reduce stress to reduce our cravings.

So far we have talked about:
1. The connection between sleep, stress and sugar cravings
2. Meditation
3. Exercise and movement
4. To-do and not-to-do lists

Today we add **'Self-care',** what does self-care mean to you?
A massage, a walk, a swim, a trip out with friends, read a book?

Do what works for you but do it with compassion, not self-criticism. What would you advise your friend to do, in a loving supportive way? That is how you should support yourself.

Maybe try the 3, 5, 8 breath technique:

You breathe in through your nose and you breathe out through your mouth.

You'll breathe in for 3, then you hold your breath for 5, then you breathe out for 8.

When you breathe out longer than you breathe in the information your body is getting is that you are safe, you can relax.

You need to do 4 cycles of this breath any time you feel stress coming up.

Sugar free Life

Stages on Your Journey
Lesson 15

I would like to invite you today to go in, connect with yourself to see how you are. How is this sugar-free journey going for you?

We all go through the stages on this journey and today I would like to make you aware of the stages, so you can recognise them and move on.

The stages are not rigid. You can miss some, or you can go through the stages in any order. It is not the same for everybody.

Today I want you to be aware of the stages:

1. Discovery – That is the stage where everybody's happy. You like it. You're finding it easy.

2. Resistance – where nothing makes sense, it doesn't work, you don't like it, you are saying to yourself: this is never going to work. It's too simple. It's too stupid. You may get angry and resentful. Keep going you are making progress.

3. Curiosity and awareness – You are starting to recognise Why are you going for sugar. You are slowly starting to recognise your triggers, making connections between your behaviour, your triggers and sugar cravings. Be kind this is good.

4. Acceptance – You know this is a journey. You know there are ups and downs but also you know you have tools to deal with challenges. You also know that nobody is perfect including you. Well done, keep it up, you're doing great.

5. Change –Your relationship with food is no longer a problem anymore. Food is not an enemy. You know difficult times will come, that's life, but you have a set of tools to work with. Well done, you have made it, carry on.

Sugar free Life

WEEK 4

Day 22 Practice, Practice

Repetition for Success
Review Day

It is a revision day again so please go back to the videos and transcriptions from last week and keep practising. Like any other habit, your new routine gets easier over time.

It is possible to make it effortless. I have seen it many times. The only way to make that happen is to make it a habit and to learn how to deal with cravings.

I would like to congratulate you for being here with me for 3 weeks.
If you didn't take any sugar for all this time it is a big achievement, well done!!

If you couldn't resist sugar a few times I congratulate you anyway because you are still here. That means you want to do it.

You might need some support to help you stay on track. You can call a friend or you can get in touch with me. I would love to help you. Sometimes it is about accountability partner, or you might need to work on your emotional eating. It is not easy to work on that on your own. It is OK to ask for help.

Here is the link to book 30 minutes session with me:
https://calendly.com/greenmindfulketo/30min

Sugar free Life

My Notes Week 3

Day 23 Me Time

Rest, plan and reassess

Let's get ready for success in week 4

Top Tips from week 3

- Put yourself first for a week
- Plan 'me time'
- Practice breathing exercises
- Note the emotions that make you feel 'hungry'
- Do something else if you need to or call a friend
- Meal plan for next week
- Shop for next week
- Keep going, you are doing great

Today I only would like you do 1 job - meal plan for next week.
It is best to do it in the morning and then enjoy the rest of the day.
Do something you really love.
Think about this as a recharging day.
Please don't go to finish your work.
Don't read your emails.
It is important to rest and have fun otherwise you can't keep going.

Sugar free Life

Week 4 - My Shopping List

Week 4 Food Diary

Download the 7 Day Sample Meal Plan - Then write here what you actually had

Day 1

Breakfast

Lunch

Dinner

Day 2

Breakfast

Lunch

Dinner

Day 3

Breakfast

Lunch

Dinner

Day 4

Breakfast

Lunch

Dinner

Sugar free Life

Week 4 Food Diary

Be honest about what you actually had

Day 5

Breakfast

Lunch

Dinner

Day 6

Breakfast

Lunch

Dinner

Day 7

Breakfast

Lunch

Dinner

My Notes

Be honest, note everything, sit down to eat, focus on your meals, eat only what is on the recommended list

Day 24 Food 4

Three Meals a Day and IF
Lesson 16

Timing of the meals and intermittent fasting.

I would like you to have only 3 meals a day, no snacking. Why?

- It gives the body a chance to repair

- Eating well three times a day reduces the temptation to snack

- Not eating between 8pm and 8am means a 12 hour fast for your body to heal and recharge

- Never eat less than 3 hours before bedtime, this is not good for your health or waistline

- Brush your teeth around 8pm, it may put you off late night snacking

- Keep out of the kitchen (and don't ask others to bring you food!)

- Remember all of the techniques already learned for avoiding cravings and giving in to emotional eating

- Write your journal in the evening and make a note of how well you are doing

Day 25 Cravings 4

EFT - The Emotional Freedom Technique
Lesson 17

If you have any cravings, which probably you do, it's going to be about emotional eating.

Today is all about the **Emotional Freedom Technique** (known as tapping)

We all want to stop eating sugar, but in order to change the behaviour for good, we need to work on what's behind the behaviour, which are our limiting beliefs, our emotions, all of those that we learn to suppress, put it down, leave it for later and not feeling it. What are we doing here is bringing that up, feeling the feelings and dealing with it. Sometimes it's enough just to let them be with you and they disappear. But sometimes those thoughts and feelings are with us a little bit longer. It depends.

So just one more time, you cannot avoid facing your emotions, gremlins, demons. There is no shortcut. We need to face them. It is hard at the beginning. I'm not going to lie but the more you do it, the easier it gets.

Watch the video with Ivana in todays lesson as often as you need to understand this technique and how it can help you.

The script for Tapping for food cravings is on the next pages.

Sugar free Life

Day 25 Cravings 4
Tapping for food cravings script

SUDS Level Before Tapping

SUDS Level After Tapping

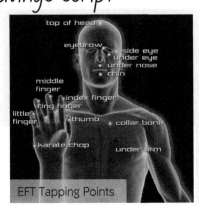

Even though I have a craving for …. I (love)
and accept myself anyway x 3

This craving for …
This desire
I want it
It makes me FEEL GOOD
So yummy
I can't have it so I want it more
One won't hurt
I'll just have a little bit
Doesn't count if no one sees
This one doesn't count if I don't write it down
I've already started so have to keep eating
I've broken my plan now, so what the hell
I'll eat it now
I have no willpower when it comes to this food
If it's in the house, I can't resist
I'll always struggle with this food
This gives me time out
These sugary foods are the only sweetness in my life
I've got to have it
I'm excited to eat this
I'm salivating
It looks so tasty/sweet/salty/fatty/sugary
It smells so nice
So creamy/soft/smooth/crunchy
So hot/warm/cool
It makes me feel loved

Day 25 Cravings 4

Tapping for food cravings script continued

I feel like I need to eat the whole thing
I've always eaten this
I will always eat this food
Who cares
Who cares I'm fat anyway
Who cares, I'll never be thin
Who cares, I'll never be able to be free of this food so why try
I am a sweet tooth/chocaholic/savoury person/sugar addict
I don't want to deal with what's behind eating this food I crave
Eating this makes me feel special
I need this to feel full
I'll feel deprived if I don't have this
It's not fair if I don't have this
Other people get away with it and I don't
I don't know what would happen if I didn't have this
I feel less stressed/anxious/upset about what's going on when I eat it
I'm so tired/busy/have a lot to do, and this will give me energy/keep me awake
Good childhood memories – food is fun, carefree, celebration
Bad childhood memories – food is a calming, distracting, commiseration
I'm not hungry, but I want it anyway
I know it's not healthy, but I want it anyway
I know it will stop weight loss, but I want it anyway
I know it will make me gain weight, but I want it anyway
I know I will feel bad after, but I want it anyway
I'll start again on Monday
This pleasure makes life bearable
Eating this food is part of life
I don't want to stop right now, I just want to eat it.
I have to eat it all, I've paid for it
Where are you now 1-10
I might be open to the possibility that I can change
I might find another way to feel better
This food is never going to really help
I choose to feel calm and relaxed
I choose to stay in control
I could have this feeling any time I want

Day 25 Cravings 4
Tapping for food cravings script continued

It is just food
It doesn't have feelings
And it certainly can't make me happy
I choose to be in control
I can have food at any time I want
it is easy to find other ways to relax
take a deep breath

where are you now 1-10
give it a little nibble and see where are you?
Even though ….
Notice what specifically you still like
Even though I still crave ….. I completely love and except myself x3
makes me so happy, good …
I don't want to give that up
I am not giving that up
I refuse to give that up
Don't take away my happiness
Don't take away my excitement
That …
I just love it soo much
I wonder who I could give this feeling to
So it is not living in my food
Keep tapping
Visualise all that feelings out of … and bring it in your heart, bring all those feelings.
Now think of the person that you want to give this feelings to. (if there
is no person imagine a tree or to yourself- younger self)
Give the person all those feeling as a ball of light
Notice how much she loves it
then she is sending to you and back and forth
taste it in your mind
Taste it again

Sugar free Life

Day 26 Mindfulness 4

The The 7 Steps of Mindful Eating
Lesson 18

Today we put all of the seven steps together. So if you don't have food in front of you, please stop the video, or reading this and make yourself something to eat and either join me and watch the video or print off the list and start practicing.

I recommend you print this list and keep practicing until mindful eating becomes your new habit. It is a very powerful practice. It will give you better results than any diet you have ever tried before. Practice daily!

7 STEPS OF MINDFUL EATING

1. Before you start eating check in and **rate how hungry you are from 1-10**.

2. Sit down and **remove distractions**

3. **Look at your food and notice** is it attractive? - Have you started salivating or not? Digestion starts in your brain.

4. **Stress level** - we can't digest food when we are in the stress response. Become aware of your stress level. Do not start eating while you feel stressed.

5. **Breath - prayer - relaxing effect**. Use your preferred breathing exercise to reduce stress.

6. If you are relaxed start **eating - SLOWLY.** Try to chew your food and pay attention to the taste, smell - BE WITH THIS FOOD.

7. Check in and ask the question **Am I still hungry?** Imagine a blender to help you achieve your goal. When you stop being hungry STOP eating. Do not wait to feel full.

Sugar free Life

Day 27 Stress 4

Boundaries and Heart Focused Breathing
Lesson 19

We are close to the end of the course and I hope you can now see the connections between stress and your sugar cravings. Have you noticed how there is nothing wrong with you? You don't have a willpower problem. You are just not perfect, which means you are human.

In week 1 we talked about **sleep, stress and sugar craving connection**, in week 2, **movement and exercise**. In week 3 we talked about **self-care.** Today is about **Boundaries**.

Are you a people pleaser, a you pleaser? Do you find it hard to say no so say yes when you don't want to? This extra breathing technique may help you to step back and think before you make a decision, and may help you to say no when you need to. Boundaries, your truth, is important for your success and self care.

Heart Focused Breathing

This type of breathing significantly reduces stress and helps connect the heart and the mind.

The first step is just breathing a little bit deeper and a little bit longer than before.

Then focus on your chest area. You can even put your hand on your heart and imagine breathing in through the heart and breathing out through the heart? Stay there for a few breaths.

Step number three is to imagine something that brings love into your heart. It could be a person, a place, a memory. Find something that is going to make you feel appreciation, love, understanding.

Then just keep breathing in and out through your heart while you keep the picture of whatever brings love into your heart.

Sugar free Life

Day 28 Habits 4

What to do Next
Lesson 20

Congratulation on being here. Well done! You proved that you can do this.

It wasn't an easy thing to do. I know that you have tried to stay away from sugar many times before. You would be successful for a while and then go back to eating sugar. WHY?

In my opinion, it is because you wanted to be perfect. That is impossible. The missing part was understanding why you fail and what to do about it.

In this course, **I showed you how to fail and how to get back on your feet. Failing is a part of learning.**

I showed you techniques you can use when the craving comes. Sometimes none of those works. The key at that moment is to have compassion and love for yourself. When you find love in your heart for all your parts you can keep going without shame and blame.

You have tools to deal with cravings now and when you fail you simply start again the next day. Over time you will have less and less of those episodes.

Now, could you go back to the questionnaire you've done at the beginning of the course and review it and complete the final part of the questionnaire on the next pages.

So what is next? Check out the hints and tips at the end of the questionnaire.

Sugar free Life

Questionnaire

After the Course

Have you noticed improvements in . . .

34. Your digestion?

35. Your sleep?

36. Your energy levels?

37. The exercise you take?

38. Your stress levels?

39. Any mood swings?

40. Brain fog?

41. Your food allergies?

42. Your depression?

43. Changes in your cycle?

44. Bowel habits?

45. Did you learn to eat slower?

46. How have these changes affected you?

Sugar free Life

Questionnaire

After the Course continued . . .

47. What did you eat for breakfast during the course?

48. When was breakfast time?

49. What did you eat for lunch during the course?

50. When was lunch time?

51. What did you eat for dinner during the course?

52. When was dinner time?

53. Did you eat snacks during the course?

Your notes on the changes since you started the course

Sugar free Life

What is Next

Moving forward sugar free

It can take 90 days to form a habit. Continually revisit this workbook and your online daily videos to help you to stay on track.

These 2 pointers may also be useful for you . . .

1. To stay sugar-free you need your tribe.

You need people around you who are doing the same thing. Otherwise, it's really hard to stay away from sugar or to do anything just on your own.

I would like you to make a list of people who are making you feel better and a list of the people who are draining you.

Try to do your best to stay around people who are actually inspiring you, who are eating healthy, living healthy, and then it's going to be much easier for you to do the same.

 2**. I would like to invite you to join my FB group:**

https://www.facebook.com/groups/fromketotodietless

If you feel that you can continue on your own well done. Congratulations!

3. In case you have some issues that you really couldn't clear on your own and you need support/help with please book a session with me.

Here is the link: https://calendly.com/greenmindfulketo/15min

Thank you for being here with me and I wish you a sugar-free life.

Sugar free Life

My Notes

Sugar *free* Life

My Notes

My Notes

My Notes

Printed in Great Britain
by Amazon

25672770R00044